Original title:
Galaxy Gossip

Copyright © 2025 Creative Arts Management OÜ
All rights reserved.

Author: Tobias Sterling
ISBN HARDBACK: 978-1-80567-851-9
ISBN PAPERBACK: 978-1-80567-972-1

Cosmic Currents

In the depths of space, stars collide,
Whispering secrets, with nowhere to hide.
Comets giggle as they zoom past,
While planets in orbit share stories so fast.

Saturn's rings, a glittering show,
Jupiter's moons all in a row.
Mars tells a joke, but it's cheeky,
Earth rolls its eyes, saying, 'You're sneaky!'

Black holes are known for their parties,
Where gravity pulls in all the hearties.
Asteroids dance, with a wobble and spin,
While aliens chuckle, shouting, 'Let's begin!'

Nebulas blush, in colors so bright,
As starlight twinkles, like a wink in the night.
Light years away, laughter echoes around,
In the cosmic neighborhood, joy can be found.

Whispering Worlds

Twinkling stars trade silly tales,
While planets sing of playful gales.
Comets giggle in a cosmic race,
Saturn's rings in a jolly embrace.

Jupiter's storms hold a raucous dance,
Neptune's winds join in the prance.
Mars winks at Earth with a cheeky glow,
While Black Holes burp, putting on a show.

Deep Space Stories

Asteroids joke about their weight,
Saying, "It's tough to find a date!"
While moons swap secrets of starry nights,
With playful nudges and cosmic flights.

Shooting stars wish for a bigger role,
Hoping for moments that are out of control.
Alien life laughs at our strange ways,
Finding our selfies just a bit queasy haze.

Tales from the Celestial Sea

In the depths where stardust flows,
Creatures giggle in shining rows.
Octopus Nebula spins around,
Telling tales without a sound.

Cosmic whales do acrobatics in space,
Chasing moonbeams at a thrilling pace.
Silly little froggies on distant stars,
Make up legends of Venusian bars.

Midnight Musings

Meteor showers throw a party,
Dancing with rocks both sharp and hearty.
A gala where Martians share their glee,
Snacking on snacks from the Milky Way tea.

Eclipses poke fun at the sun's bright face,
While Saturn throws confetti with grace.
And as the night sky winks and flirts,
The universe laughs in its cosmic skirts.

Starlit Whispers

Stars giggle in their dance,
Twinkling bright with every glance.
Planets tease with playful spins,
As comets rush, collecting sins.

The moon winks with a knowing grin,
While asteroids trade tales of kin.
Black holes laugh at their own jokes,
Swirling round like playful folks.

Cosmic Chatter

In the void, a voice does beam,
Making light of every dream.
Starlings of space tell silly tales,
While meteors tell of their misfails.

Venus and Mars exchange good cheers,
Sharing secrets through the years.
Galaxies swipe like they're online,
Making memes with stellar shine.

Celestial Secrets

Whispers float on solar winds,
Rocketing off like playful sins.
Planets gossip in a loop,
As stardust sparkles in a scoop.

Galactic tales of love and war,
Supernovae throwing a dance floor.
Light-years can't hold back the jokes,
As black holes stifle their pokes.

Nebulae Narratives

Clouds of color swirl and sway,
Spinning yarns in a vibrant way.
Stars trade stories under wraps,
While comets plot their funny mishaps.

Whirling dust makes quite the scene,
Dancing bright in cosmic sheen.
Asteroids chuckle in a row,
Creating tales that steal the show.

Celestial Soliloquies

Stars have secrets, oh so bright,
Whispered tales in the dead of night.
Planets giggle in their orbits wide,
While comets chuckle, swift to glide.

Asteroids argue, what a sight,
Debating who shines the most in flight.
Each nebula bursts with colors bold,
Sharing jokes from the ages old.

Stellar Speculations

Venus swears it knows the score,
While Mars just claims it sees more.
Saturn laughs with rings in tow,
"Bet I can spin faster, you know!"

Jupiter's storms all join the fun,
"Who's ready for a cosmic run?"
Uranus giggles, can't contain,
"Not everything's serious in the main!"

Intergalactic Intrigues

Aliens sip on starry brews,
Exchanging rumors, sharing views.
Black holes grinning, they're such trolls,
Pulling pranks on wandering souls.

Light-years away, the laughter flows,
As supernovas strike silly poses.
Cosmic entities unite in jest,
For who says space can't be the best?

Cometary Chitchat

Comets streak and weave about,
Making snappy remarks, no doubt.
"Did you hear what that quasar said?,"
"Something funny that's gone to bed!"

Each passing star has tales to share,
About the moon's latest wild hair.
With laughter echoing in the void,
They surely keep their humor employed.

Celestial Observations

Stars whispering tales quite bold,
They gossip of comets, smug and old.
Planets chuckle, spinning round,
While asteroids dance without a sound.

Nebulas giggle, colors so bright,
While black holes sulk, avoiding the light.
They all trade jokes, in the night air,
Lunar laughter floats everywhere.

Spacetime Shenanigans

In the void, spacemen like to tease,
Wormholes play tricks, such a breeze.
They zip and zag, from here to there,
But forgot one galactic fare!

Saturn's rings shine, what a show,
Twirling around like a disco glow.
While Martians prank with silly faces,
Creating chaos in distant places.

Universal Utterances

Cosmic rays whisper, can you believe?
The Milky Way's full of tricks up its sleeve.
Light-years apart, they share a laugh,
Spilling secrets over interstellar craft.

Supernovas pop, like confetti in space,
While aliens debate who's got the best face.
They trade cosmic rants, with much cheer,
Creating mischief from far and near.

Stygian Secrets

In shadowy depths where dark matters dwell,
Jupiter's moons plot and conspire as well.
They tuck away jokes about the sun,
Whispers of secrets, oh what fun!

Never trust a black hole's embrace,
It promises worlds, yet leaves no trace.
Even in darkness, laughter's a must,
For celestial beings, it's more than just dust.

Planetary Patter

In the sun's warm rays, we spin and whirl,
Jupiter's got secrets, do give him a twirl.
Mars claims he's the hottest, but what a bluff,
Venus just laughs, saying, 'That's not enough!'

Mercury whispers tales of speedy flights,
While Saturn's rings glimmer under moonlit nights.
Uranus just chuckles, says, 'I'm the odd one,'
But deep down he knows, it's all in good fun!

Orbiting Rumors

Pluto throws a party, has all the best snacks,
But tell him, he's tiny, he'll just roll his lax.
Neptune is busy, with forecasts and tides,
While the comet just zooms, it never confides.

Earth's got some gossip, it's swirling anew,
Is that really a selfie? Or a photo of dew?
The asteroid belts laugh at how they all roam,
Each one with a story, they're never alone!

Twilight Dialogues

In the shade of the stars, they gather and chat,
Venus and Mars, in a cosmic spat.
'Oh please, you're old news,' Venus giggles with glee,
While Mars flexes muscles, saying, 'Look at me!'

The moons on a break, enjoying their tea,
While asteroids gossip, 'Who's next on the spree?'
'What do you think of that bright shooting star?'
'He's just showing off, he won't travel far!'

Infinite Echoes

Across the vast void, the echoes resound,
'Who's that singing? Oh, it's just Space Hound!'
Black holes hum softly, secrets they keep,
While comets run wild, they don't dare to sleep.

A supernova chatters, 'I'm the life of the show!'
While distant galaxies wave, 'Put on a glow!'
The universe laughs, in a syncopated beat,
With every new star, another tale to repeat!

Starbound Stories

In a nebula so bright, it seems,
Stars are spitting out wild beams.
One said, 'I'm dating a comet!'
The other laughed, 'You're such a prophet!'

Planets gather for awkward chats,
One claims he's tight with space bats.
A black hole yawned, 'I need a snack!'
And the sun just turned his back!

Celestial Chronicles

A meteor shower sparked some glee,
While asteroids danced like in a spree.
'Just don't trip!' said a wise old star,
'You'll end up bouncing near and far!'

Venus teased Mars with a wink,
'Your red is bold, but boy, you stink!'
The moons chuckled, circling on high,
As laughter echoed through the sky.

Beyond the Event Horizon

Enter if you dare, said a quirky light,
Where time flops and things just don't feel right.
Jupiter told tales of his wild ride,
While Saturn blushed and tried to hide.

A time-traveling star joined the clan,
Saying, 'Trust me, I'm my own biggest fan!'
But hiccups in time made them all dizzy,
And black holes popped up, feeling quite frizzy.

Astronomical Anecdotes

In a corner of space, shadows played,
Alien jokes that never seemed to fade.
One claimed he'd made friends with a ray,
Who said, 'I'm light years away, hey hey!'

Comets tried their best to impress,
But got tangled like hair, what a mess!
Uranus giggled, gave a green shout,
'I've got the best fart jokes—check it out!'

Celestial Secrets

Stars giggle and sparkle, they play hide and seek,
The universe whispers, oh isn't that chic!
Planets share secrets with their moons by the light,
"Did you hear what Mars said about Venus last night?"

Asteroids dance wildly like they've lost their way,
While comets flash by, bringing joy to the fray.
A black hole is laughing, it swallows with glee,
"Keep secrets from me? Oh, you'll never be free!"

Lunar Legends

The moon pulls some pranks with its silvery shine,
   Telling tales of old times, "Oh, isn't it fine?"
Rabbits hop bold, playing tricks on the stars,
   While the sun yawns and just sips from jars.

"Did you see that shooting star? What a fumble!"
   The wise old owl chuckles, "Oh, watch them tumble!"
Night critters gossip, all buzzing with cheer,
   "What's new in the cosmos? Come on, let's hear!"

Nebula Narratives

Clouds of color swirl, weaving tales in delight,
"Did you catch the latest? It's a meteor sight!"
Gas giants chuckle, tipping their hats to the night,
"Better check your orbit, or you'll lose the light!"

Little stars wink, sharing stories of old,
Hilarious happenings that never get told.
A supernova bursts, lighting up the place,
"Can you believe that? It's now a big race!"

Stellar Stories

In the dark of space, laughter echoes so bright,
Celestial beings revel in sheer delight.
Galactic beings gossip, spinning yarns with great flair,
"Did you hear about Pluto? It's thinking of a dare!"

Twinkling tales float by on cosmic winds,
"Neptune's got a weird dance, a twist that transcends!"
All the stars chuckle, as they wink and they nod,
The universe is silly, isn't that quite odd?

Cosmic Crux

In the Milky Way, stars exchange tales,
A comet forgot its way—oops, it derails!
Nebulae giggle, filling the space,
As black holes chuckle, losing their grace.

Asteroids trade snacks, all out of sight,
While planets debate who's the fastest in flight.
Saturn's rings shine bright, like disco balls,
Mars claims it's the coolest, but nobody calls.

Quasar Queries

Quasars in laughter, lighting the night,
Pulsars spin stories, oh what a sight!
"Who needs gravity?" says a brave little star,
"I'm bouncing around, I'll go far—so far!"

Alien chitchat, gossiping fast,
"Did you see Pluto? It just went past!"
Cosmic winds carrying whispers abound,
While titans in space, dance round and round.

Cosmic Connection

Mars texts Venus, "What's up with the dust?"
While Jupiter laughs, "Just chill, that's a must!"
Neptune's got jokes, but they fall flat,
As Uranus giggles, "Is it me, or is that?"

Stardust debates on who's cooler tonight,
"Let's gather some meteors, let's hang tight!"
In the great expanse, friendships ignite,
Over light-years they laugh, oh what a delight!

Whispered in the Void

Whispers in space, like a breeze through the dark,
"Did you see that? A shooting star's spark!"
Asteroids gossip, "Did you hear the news?"
Comets crack up in vibrant hues.

Galaxies winking, sharing a joke,
While cosmic dust dances, an invisible cloak.
Stars rolling their eyes, "It's all just a phase,"
In the grand cosmos, they spend their days.

Midnight Murmurs

Stars whisper tales, oh so bright,
Planets giggle through the night.
Comets race with fevered glee,
Asteroids dance, won't let it be.

Black holes grumble, 'Oh not again!'
Caught in a star's fiery den.
Nebulas chuckle in pastel hues,
While meteors trade their cosmic news.

Saturn's rings, a twisted prank,
Jupiter's storms, they fill the tank.
Venus winks, sees all the fuss,
While Mars just laughs in the cosmic bus.

In this cosmic cafe, with a sigh,
The Milky Way always passing by.
Galactic jesters, hear them chime,
Celestial giggles, oh what a time!

Milky Way Murmurs

In the lanes of starlit lanes,
Whispers of quarks play silly games.
Wormholes wink, oh what a tease,
Lightyears stretch with cosmic ease.

Planets trade their fashion tips,
While moons toss snacks from their ships.
Orion's belt, a fashion fail,
And Venus jokes, 'I do not ail.'

Asteroids meet in wild debate,
'Who's the fastest on this rate?'
Galaxies spin with too much sass,
While stardust giggles, 'Let's not pass!'

Cosmic buddies in their own way,
Laughing through the endless play.
Stars collide with a wink and poke,
In this universe, it's all a joke!

Twilight Tattletales

Dusk brings whispers from afar,
Twinkling tales of a shooting star.
Nebulae gossip in drying light,
While meteors plot mischief tonight.

Pulsars nod, they're in the loop,
Trading secrets with a happy group.
Galactic wanderers stop and stare,
As cosmic jesters weave their snare.

Stars gather 'round for a good chat,
While planets giggle, that's where it's at!
'Did you hear what Venus said?'
Laughter echoes, filling the spread.

In this twilight of merry jest,
Cosmic mischief, it's the best!
From black holes to sentient dust,
In the universe we simply trust!

Pulsar Parables

In a starry bistro, lights aglow,
Pulsars spin tales, don't you know?
Quasars pop in with a loud cheer,
Every light year brings a new leer.

Astrologers ponder on their chairs,
While meteors share their wild affairs.
Constellations, oh what's the scoop?
Twinkling tales of the interstellar group.

Mars equipped with a funny hat,
Saturn sings, imagine that!
Chasing stars with a joyful grin,
Cosmic humor, let the fun begin!

In the fabric of space, laughter flows,
Cosmic clerks hear the gossip grows.
With every twinkle, each fun detail,
Galactic puns set the universe on sale!

Cosmic Conversations

Stars whisper secrets in the night,
Planets giggle, what a sight!
Black holes laugh at their own fate,
While satellites gossip, oh so late!

Nebulas exchange tales so bright,
About shooting stars that take flight.
Comets dance with a silly flair,
As asteroids shrug without a care!

Stellar Slip-ups

Mars mistook Venus for a snack,
Jupiter tripped, but never looked back.
Saturn's rings had a fashion fight,
While Uranus joked, 'Who's out tonight?'

The sun spilled coffee on its ray,
While stars played hide and seek all day.
Moon quipped, 'I'm no one's satellite!'
As comets zoomed with sheer delight!

Interstellar Insights

A white dwarf thinks it's so wise,
But supernovae just roll their eyes.
Planets share their most silly dreams,
Like black holes' wild and wobbly schemes!

Aliens giggle from afar,
At Earthlings arguing 'bout who's bizarre.
Star clusters trade their best jokes,
While space dust drifts, a cloud of folks!

Comet Tales

The comets brought tales from the edge,
With ice cream cones made of pure wedge.
They painted the skies with trails of cheer,
While galaxies giggled, loud enough to hear!

In space, it's all laughter and light,
Where stardust dances throughout the night.
Planets wink in a cosmic play,
As meteors zoom and drift away!

Astro Avowals

Stars twinkled brightly in the night,
While comets raced with endless delight.
Mars whispered secrets, oh so sly,
As Venus laughed, 'Did you see that guy?'

Black holes gossiped in a swirling dance,
Planets chuckled at their cosmic chance.
Jupiter boasted, 'I've got the most moons!'
While Saturn smirked, 'Count my rings, very prunes!'

Neptune said, 'I'm cooler, don't you know?'
But Uranus chimed in, 'I steal the show!'
Their laughter echoed through the vast space,
A silly bouquet of starlit grace.

In this vastness, fun are the stars,
Sharing their tales from nearby and far.
So join the party, don't be a bore,
In this cosmic chatter, there's always more!

Celestial Myths

Once upon a time in the night sky,
A shooting star gave a wink and a sigh.
It told of aliens with dance moves grand,
Who tangled with creatures from a far-off land.

The moon chuckled softly, 'What nonsense, my friend!'
While the sun rolled his eyes, 'Shall we pretend?'
Constellations snickered below their haze,
As meteors took turns in a silly craze.

Mercury, speedy, had tales to share,
Of racing across with the grace of a hare.
Pluto piped up, 'Hey, I'm still in the game!'
But the others just laughed, 'That's quite a claim!'

In this celestial realm of make-believe,
Funny stories are what we conceive.
Join the mirth of the cosmic lore,
With each twinkling star, there's always more!

Astronomical Allegiances

The planets gathered for a lighthearted fuss,
To decide who should travel on the next bus.
Earth said, 'I'll take the humans, alright!'
While Mars grinned wide, 'I'll bring snacks for the flight!'

Venus dressed up in a sparkling gown,
While Saturn spun rings and laughed like a clown.
'Are you ready?' called out bright little stars,
'We'll race through the night, past Venus and Mars!'

The meteors zoomed, shouting, 'Who's got the speed?'
'We'll win this adventure, just follow our lead!'
As asteroids chuckled, creating a scene,
In their cosmic joke, they felt so supreme.

Galactic alliances were formed with delight,
In this universe where laughter takes flight.
So, buckle up tight, for fun is in store,
In the laughter of space, there's always more!

Cosmic Clues

Come gather, dear stargazers, lend me your ear,
For cosmic clues that will bring you good cheer.
A red giant bragged, 'I'm the biggest in town!'
While a dwarf star sneered, 'I won't wear that crown!'

In a playful whisper, a meteor went,
'The stars are just gossiping; I think it's a trend!'
Neptune shook with laughter, 'Can't hold it back!'
As Pluto chimed in, 'I feel so out of whack!'

Comet tails swirled with giggles so sweet,
While the Milky Way danced on whimsical feet.
The universe buzzed with bright, silly tales,
Of moons and of planets with mismatched scales.

So if you're feeling down, just look up at night,
For the skies are a canvas, painted with light.
Join in this laughter, let worries implore,
In this celestial sphere, there's always more!

Aurora Anecdotes

In the skies where colors play,
Dancing lights have much to say.
Stars whisper tales of silly fuss,
While planets giggle on their bus.

A comet's comet tells a joke,
"Why did the star become a bloke?
Because he needed space to shine!"
The moon just honked, "That one's mine!"

Dwarf planets laugh, a merry band,
They can't believe they're not in demand.
"Too small to twinkle, too big to cry,
Still making waves, oh my, oh my!"

Cosmic beans spill laughter bright,
As asteroids dance with all their might.
So let's toast to space, the cosmic floor,
Where every twinkle is never a bore!

Radiant Rumors

A shooting star's a glitzy tease,
Whispering secrets with a breeze.
"Did you hear about that blue dwarf?"
"They're just a big star, trying to morph!"

Saturn's rings have recipes,
For swirling snacks that tease and please.
"Make sure you add a pinch of flair,
Or else it's just a solar scare!"

Lunar landers strut about,
Spilling shadows, boasting loud.
"I flew to Mars, didn't you see?
But came back home, too wild for me!"

Meteor showers rave with glee,
Circling tales of cosmic spree.
"Who grabbed that star? What a sight!"
Such radiant whispers fill the night!

Constellation Chatter

Beneath the stars, they bicker and grin,
Ursa Major just bumped into her twin.
"Keep your distance, don't steal my light,"
While Orion moans, "I'm losing this fight!"

Canis Major barked a silly tune,
"Why did the planet visit the moon?
To fetch a cheese that's aged and bright!
They claim it's a cosmic delight!"

And Venus chimes in with a wink,
"I hear Martians love to drink pink!"
Rumors swirl like stardust, you see,
While Cassiopeia adjusts with glee.

Stars trade jests—no time for tears,
Making memories through centuries, not years.
So here's to the night, with all its flair,
Where constellations laugh without a care!

Spherical Secrets

In the heart of space, where wonders float,
A planet jokes about his coat.
"Too hot for me, I'd rather chill,"
While a nearby star just can't sit still!

Black holes gossip, swirling fate,
"Have you seen how they dance late?"
With solar flares that wave and prance,
It's a wild cosmic game of chance!

Jupiter snickers at his moons,
Playing leapfrog, they hum their tunes.
"Watch us zoom! We travel far!"
While Earth just rolls her eyes, bizarre.

Comets burst with tales on trails,
Of outlandish shipwork and ridiculous sails.
Spherical secrets in endless jest,
A universe of laughter, truly the best!

Astral Anecdotes

Stars are whispering, oh what a tale,
Black holes hiccuping, they just can't bail.
Comets are sneezing, flying through space,
While aliens giggle, a cosmic embrace.

Nebulas painting, with colors so bright,
Saturn's rings laughing, what a funny sight!
Meteor showers, like clowns on parade,
In the vast universe, jokes are well-made.

Mars is grumbling, 'Why's Earth so loud?'
Venus is pouting, feeling left out.
Jupiter's swirling, tossing out jest,
In the cosmic chaos, we're laughing the best.

So grab a telescope, join in the fun,
In this endless dance, we shine like the sun.
Amongst the twinkling, let laughter take flight,
In the grand expanse, joy lights up the night.

Planetary P Gossip

Pluto's pouting, 'Am I still in the club?'
Mercury's speeding, it just can't stub.
Venus is sipping, sweet cosmic tea,
Mars is telling tales, 'Just wait and see!'

Saturn's got bling, with rings all aglow,
While Neptune swims deep, where no one can go.
Earth's sharing secrets, whispers of fate,
While Jupiter's blustering, 'Just eat off my plate!'

Asteroids chat, 'Did you hear the news?'
Moons are all gossiping, sharing their views.
Galileo chuckles, 'Did you hear the sound?
That's just the universe messing around!'

Cosmic dancing, spinning with cheer,
In this wild realm, giggles are near.
Planets and moons in their whimsical ballet,
Chasing the starlight, come laugh and play!

Solar Serenades

The sun has a joke, it's lighting the way,
While planets are singing at the break of day.
Solar winds giggle, as comets fly by,
A waltz of the cosmos, oh me, oh my!

Uranus is spinning with quite the grace,
While Mercury's trotting, keeping up the pace.
The sun cracks a smile, with each solar flare,
Venus rolls her eyes, 'There's warmth in the air!'

Meanwhile, the asteroids throw a party,
Singing out loud, oh there's no need to be hearty.
'Join us and dance,' they call with delight,
In this solar ballet, jokes take their flight.

So strum on the rays, let merriment rise,
The solar system's full of joyful surprise.
In this wacky grandeur, laughter's the tune,
Under the glow of a cosmic cartoon!

Twilight Tidings

Twilight's a canvas where stars start to play,
They share all the quirks from their bustling day.
Orion's got stories, and Cassiopeia too,
While the moon winks softly, 'Oh, what's new?'

Woodland creatures now look to the skies,
As constellations sparkle, a feast for the eyes.
Shooting stars giggle, racing in flight,
Making wishes come true in the still of the night.

Galactic confetti, thrown in the air,
Comets are grinning, it's a cosmic affair.
Venus declares, 'I'm the brightest around,'
While the sun is just waiting, without making a sound.

So let's toast the heavens, with laughter and cheer,
In this twilight magic, the universe near.
With smiles and with joy, we'll spin through the light,
In the heart of this cosmos, everything's right.

Dark Sky Dialogue

In the night, stars throw shade,
Whispering secrets, unafraid.
Planets giggle with delight,
As comets dance, oh what a sight!

Forgetful moons, lost in their glow,
Swapping stories we hardly know.
Black holes chuckle, 'We eat it fast!'
While meteors rush, quite a blast!

Nebulas swirl in rainbow splats,
Stardust sings of cosmic chats.
A winking sun overheard a tale,
Of aliens trying to fly a snail!

In this vastness, laughter's key,
Eternal jokes in zero-G.
Even lightyears have their jest,
By dark humor, we are blessed.

Solar Flare Folklore

Solar flares are quite the ruckus,
Spitting fire, oh what a circus!
The sun winks, sending sparks galore,
While space folks roll on their floor.

Asteroids sharing tales at dusk,
Recounting pranks – just pure, good musk!
The stellar winds blowing laughter near,
While astrobiologists sip up their beer.

Planets moan, 'Where's my orbit gone?'
Stellar hiccups, of course, a con!
Black holes spinning yarns so tight,
To liven up the cosmic night.

Feisty Martians claim they're sleek,
While Venus giggles, "Oh, 'm so chic!"
With each solar flare, gossip streams,
Cosmic humor fuels our dreams.

Celestial Conspiracies

Whispers drift through the Milky Way,
Aliens plotting over tea they say.
Stars rolling eyes at cosmic tricks,
While planets swap their funny picks.

The moons are busy, plotting their schemes,
Comparing diets and starlit dreams.
"Did you hear?" Jupiter starts to grin,
"Saturn's rings, they just can't spin!"

Comets zooming in and out of sight,
Gossiping 'bout asteroids all night.
"Did you know?" said one with glee,
"Venus tried to schmooze with me!"

Galactic giggles echo so wide,
As time ticks by, no one can hide.
Even stardust has something to crack,
In endless tales that wink and snack.

Temporal Tales

Time's a trickster, oh what a tease,
Playing pranks with cosmic ease.
The past rows laugh and the future plays,
As spacetime dances in twisted ways.

Eons chatting, 'What's up with Earth?'
"Humans think they own the mirth!"
Black holes wink, keeping it sly,
While quasars giggle and claim, "Oh my!"

Parallel worlds told a joke so grand,
Dimensions cracking up, quite unplanned.
Each tick and tock just adds to the fun,
In the fabric of space, it's never done!

Cosmic clocks with giggles that soar,
Teasing time travelers as they explore.
With every moment, a punchline's spun,
In a universe where laughter's never shunned.

Starstruck Ramblings

In the night, stars peek and twinkle,
They gossip in silence, oh how they wrinkle.
A comet speeds by with a zany grin,
Whispers of drama in the cosmic din.

Black holes chuckle, pulling in noise,
While planets play tag like curious boys.
Saturn's rings spin tales of flair,
While the sun throws shade with a solar glare.

Meteor showers burst with delight,
As they race through the void in a sparkling flight.
Aliens chuckle at Earth's odd plight,
Hoping they find a little moonlight.

Nebulae swirl, painting skies silly,
With colors and patterns that dance quite frilly.
Stardust dreams weave through the air,
In this universe, it's all just a dare!

Cosmic Conundrums

Why do stars wear that sparkling dress?
Is it to impress, or to jest, no less?
Planets spin tales with childlike joy,
While asteroids watch like a cosmic toy.

The sun's got jokes that lighten the day,
While distant moons sip tea, chic in their way.
Galactic news travels faster than light,
Always a punchline just out of sight.

A supernova caused quite a stir,
As stars lined up to see the big blur.
Jupiter's storms are famous for laughs,
While Venus pretends to avoid all the gaffes.

Wormholes swirl, causing quite the mess,
With travelers grinning, "We love this stress!"
In the realms of space, fun never quits,
Each orbit a joke, who sits where, who spits?

Astrological Antics

The stars hold secrets in their bright gaze,
While planets giggle in a cosmic maze.
A sly Sagittarius tips a sly wink,
And Capricorn wonders, "What do you think?"

Pisces swims deep in dreamy delight,
While Leo roars laughter, a marvelous sight.
Aries jumps in with a daring dance,
In this zodiac party, take a chance!

Gemini twins breed banter that's sly,
While Virgo cleans up, asking "Oh why?"
Libra weighs the fun with charm on a scale,
As Scorpio plots an outrageous tale.

Shoot for the stars with a chuckling grin,
In the cosmic dance, let the laughter begin.
Astrology's antics brighten the night,
With humor and joy taking glorious flight!

Orbiting Overtones

In orbits, we spin, around and around,
Gravity's pull is a curious sound.
Planets exchange jokes in their merry dance,
As celestial bodies take a wild chance.

Mars brags about his dusty red hue,
While Earth rolls her eyes at the things he'll do.
Venus whispers stories of love in the air,
While moons just giggle without a care.

Asteroids chuckle, a rogue little crew,
Zooming past stars, they've got things to do.
Each cosmic tale a whimsical spin,
In this universe filled with laughter and grin.

As the comets race by with dramatic flair,
The cosmos is filled with gossip and flair.
Orbiting overtones echo above,
In the vastness of space, there's plenty of love!

Starfall Stories

Stars are falling like candy bars,
Whispers travel from Mars to ours.
Comets giggle while shooting by,
Space squirrels try to say hi.

Planets roll in a cosmic dance,
Some moons are caught in a silly trance.
A star named Fred wore a funny hat,
And laughed out loud—can you imagine that?

Asteroids joke about their weight,
Claiming they're just on an endless date.
The Milky Way is a gossip mill,
Spilling secrets it writes at will.

So if you listen while stargazing bright,
You might hear tales that tickle your sight.
The universe is one big tease,
With punchlines spun like cosmic breeze.

Interstellar Idiosyncrasies

In a far-off realm where oddities play,
Neptune wears shoes for a funky sway.
Saturn spins yarns that make everyone grin,
While Jupiter's storms just laugh at the din.

Aliens take tea with a side of cake,
Debating on whether to bake or forsake.
Each planet's quirks, a story untold,
Of fluffy space cats and aliens bold.

The sun likes to gossip about its own rays,
Sharing tales of night and the moon's lost days.
Stars play poker in stellar retreats,
Betting on meteors and cosmic feats.

When a black hole yawns, it's a great affair,
Sucking in gossip like it doesn't care.
The universe giggles at all the fun,
In this swirling circus known as the run.

Etheric Echoes

Echoes of laughter bounce through the void,
As space puns are made, fully enjoyed.
Blasting off jokes from Earth to the moon,
Galactic comedians sing a merry tune.

Wormholes whisper of secrets so grand,
While shooting stars offer a helping hand.
Astro-mice scurry without any care,
Nibbling on cheese in the weightless air.

Galaxy fairies trade quirky lines,
Spreading tales of buttered cosmic shrines.
Gravity tries to keep it all down,
But with laughter, it's hard to not clown.

So find a nebula to share some cheer,
And listen closely, everything's clear.
With echoes that tickle your funny bone,
The universe sings—you're never alone.

Cosmic Catchphrases

Catchphrases flicker in the starry expanse,
"Don't be a meteor, take a chance!"
Quasars are rapping about cosmic delight,
While black holes dance with a gravitational bite.

"Stay bright, like a star with a big ol' grin!"
Is the motto of comets zipping within.
Dust bunnies laugh at their fluffy attire,
While rogue planets jump, breaking all the wire.

"Float like a feather, spin like a fan,"
Says the moon while doing its best to plan.
Cosmic catchphrases become interstellar trends,
Making the universe giggle with friends.

So next time you gaze at the night sky so wide,
Remember the humor that's circling high tide.
For every twinkle and sparkle you see,
Is a catchphrase waiting for you to decree.

Comet's Confession

In a tail of glitter, I zoom and I race,
But oh, what a mess on this cosmic face!
I tripped on a star, oh what a blunder!
Now I'm dodging the jokes like a cosmic thunder!

I thought I was slick, a real shooting star,
But missed the big party at Mars' favorite bar.
They laughed from the rings, oh what a sight!
I swirled and I twirled, then vanished from light!

My friends sent invites through light-years of space,
But I misread 'now' as 'whenever, just race!'
So here I confess, with no pride, just cheer,
I always arrive a light-year too near!

But I'll bring them cake made of stardust and dreams,
And maybe they'll giggle at all of my schemes.
In the vastness of night, with a wink and a grin,
I'll show them my tricks and let the fun begin!

Eclipsed Echoes

The sun played tricks in a shadowy game,
While planets all whispered, calling my name.
"Oh moon, do tell, what secrets you keep?"
As shadows flew past, the rumors went deep.

From Venus to Saturn, the gossip was bright,
"Did you see Jupiter's new rings? Quite a sight!"
Mercury chimed, "Oh, that's fake news for sure!"
As laughter erupted in the cosmic tour!

One star even claimed it saw Mars in a dance,
Waltzing with comets, oh what a romance!
But truth be told, it was just a big joke,
As stardust and laughter in harmony woke.

So gather around, let the night play its part,
With echoes of fun that will warm every heart.
In the dark of the void, where we twinkle and beam,
We'll spin tales of mischief, like a wild cosmic dream!

Interstellar Insights

I floated through space with a curious chip,
When a quasar winked, saying, "Come take a trip!"
"See cosmic wonders and interstellar sights,
But mind your step—dodge the mischievous lights!"

From black holes with secrets to supernova cheers,
I gathered the whispers of countless light years.
"Why do stars wink?" asked a curious moon,
"Because we've got secrets to share—but not soon!"

Nearby, a nebula giggled with flair,
"Just wait till you see Mars's neon paint hair!"
And so the adventures in laughter took flight,
With aliens chuckling throughout the night.

So hold on tight, for the cosmos is grand,
With playful treasures that tickle your hand.
A swirling delight that's endless and bright,
Bringing cosmic joy in the laughter of night!

Celestial Chatter

In the realm of the stars, the chatter is keen,
Comets and asteroids share the latest scene.
"Did you spot Earth's selfies? They're quite the craze!
With filters and angles that leave us amazed!"

And Venus rolled laughter, "Oh, what a pose!
I'd flaunt my own pics, but no sunlight glows."
While Saturn spun tales from rings made of ice,
"Let's have a photo-off, oh wouldn't that be nice?"

The universe bustled with quirky delights,
As meteors danced through the star-spangled nights.
"Time for a meme!" shouted Mercury with glee,
As he crafted the best cosmic comedy!

So gather 'round friends, in the starlit parade,
Let's share our adventures and joys unafraid.
For the cosmos is vast, yet feels like a town,
Where laughter connects us, never brings us down!

Orbiting Odysseys

In a whirl of comet tails, they spin,
Joking about the stars' new skin.
"Did you hear Vega's latest prank?
He painted Betelgeuse's tank!"

Cosmic clowns in a twinkling dance,
Swapping tales of love and chance.
"Uranus wore the silliest hat,
While Earth forgot the moon was fat!"

Wormholes twist with laughter loud,
As asteroids form a giggling crowd.
"Neptune's blue is just a ruse,
He spilled some paint, now we're confused!"

Among the stardust, chuckles flow,
Freestyle orbits in a show.
With meteors bursting in mirth so bright,
The universe beams, a joyful sight!

Supernova Stories

Once a star exploded with a twist,
Spilling secrets that couldn't be missed.
"Did you see Mars on a taco night?
He danced so hard he lost his light!"

Galactic gossips with cosmic flair,
Whirling tales through the interstellar air.
"Jupiter's moons threw a wild bash,
Saturn came dressed, a total smash!"

Time travelers come for a joke or two,
Trading rumors of what's really true.
"Black holes are just wormholes that diet,
I heard that they don't want to try it!"

In this astral comedy, life's a stage,
Stars recite lines from a humor page.
With laughter echoing through the night,
Twinkles giggle in soft delight!

Starlight Secrets

Under shimmering skies, whispers conspire,
Tales of planets caught in the fire.
"Mercury lost his shades in the rush,
Venus scoffed, 'You're just a big mush!'"

A tickle of stardust, they laugh and play,
Planetary pranks lead the night's ballet.
"Pluto's back with a flip of his tail,
Saying he's just a dog with a trail!"

Astronauts eavesdrop, their giggles loud,
As stars chuckle and form a cloud.
"Did you see the moon's latest selfie?
He thought it was art, but dear, it's silly!"

With twinkling eyes, they share a joke,
Laughter rings through the cosmic cloak.
In this vast void, where fun takes flight,
Secrets twinkle, igniting the night!

Nebular Notions

In clouds of gas, rumors abound,
Floating tales swirl all around.
"Did you hear what Mars just said?
He swears he's dating a comet named Fred!"

Stars in clusters plot their schemes,
Joking about celestial dreams.
"Orions wore the latest gear,
Pretending to be hipster, oh dear!"

With nebulas laughing, colors collide,
Cosmic capers on a playful ride.
"Venus tried a spicy new line,
Got burned and now he's just fine!"

Every light-year boasts a tale to share,
Every twinkle holds laughter in the air.
Boundless joy on this ride together,
With the universe's whimsy, no matter the weather!

Starfire Secrets

In the dark, stars whisper, quite the tale,
Of cosmic pranks, and comets that rail.
Meteors giggle, skip through the night,
While moons share secrets, oh what a sight!

Black holes chuckle, they swallow with glee,
While asteroids dance, wild and free.
Planets are plotting silly little acts,
Jupiter's laughing—who's got the facts?

Twinkling winks fly from star to star,
Shooting down rumors from near and far.
Cosmic jesters, they cavort and play,
Making the night bright in a cheeky display!

Galactic giggles, what fun to behold,
In the vast, dark cosmos, stories unfold.
With twitching ends of shimmering light,
They prank the heavens, what a delight!

Orbital Observations

Take a peek through the cosmic lens,
Where space wonks gather, making amends.
They speak of orbits, and who missed a turn,
Mercury's late—oh, how we learn!

Saturn's rings are a stylish flair,
While Venus smirks, tossing back her hair.
A meteor shower? Just a firework show,
Lookers laugh as they see it glow.

Behind the telescope, quips start to brew,
A constellation fashion faux pas, who knew?
With every swirl, and wobbly spin,
The cosmos is buzzing, let the humor begin!

With stardust scattered, spacecrafts in spree,
They plot interstellar pranks, just wait and see!
Orbital mischief in the great black dome,
Making the galaxy feel like home!

Infinite Impressions

Stars paint the sky with a wink and a dash,
Creating impressions with a cosmic flash.
Supernova selfies on celestial walls,
Leaving bubbles of laughter in cosmic halls.

Planets pose in their glimmering attire,
While asteroids tumble, lost in their fire.
Neptune's small giggles cause waves all around,
While playful stardust drifts softly downbound.

Every night showcases an interstellar show,
As comets ignite the sky with their glow.
The universe chuckles as it spins and twirls,
Painting reality in pranks and whirls!

With starlight illuminating the enduring jest,
Even black holes can't help but invest.
A canvas of humor, bright as the sun,
In this endless expanse, we jest and we run!

The Celestial Conclave

Gather the planets for a roundtable meet,
Discussing their antics and who had a tweet.
Mars says he saw Venus spill her light,
A burst of laughter, oh what a plight!

The moons roll their eyes at the Earth's latest trends,
While stars exchange gossip like old-timey friends.
"A quasar joked, 'Let's give it a whirl!'
And now all the photons are starting to twirl!"

Asteroids sponsor a game called 'Fling',
Where they chuck rocks, what joy do they bring!
Neptune protests, "I'm feeling too blue!"
But the others just giggle, "We've got fun for you!"

As the cosmos chuckles, they toast with a flare,
To the scrumptious absurdity filling the air.
At the illustrious conclave, laughter won't cease,
In the grand tapestry of the universe, peace!

Ethereal Exchanges

In the stars, secrets dance so bright,
Aliens giggle, lost in the night.
Comets blush when they swoosh by,
Whispering tales from the sky.

A lunar rabbit hops in glee,
As planets play hide and seek, you see.
Saturn's rings tape the gossip's flight,
While space dust sprinkles laughter, light.

Venus winks to Mars's bold claim,
'I've got more moons, who's to blame?'
Jupiter chuckles, spinning round,
With mischief wrapped in cosmic sound.

Neptune's winds carry snickers far,
As meteors shoot like a joking star.
Ethereal exchanges in the cosmic spree,
In this universe of whimsy, we're all carefree!

Asteroid Allegories

Asteroids tumble with tales untold,
Bouncing around like they're bold.
Each rock a storyteller, quirky and small,
Cracking up with the celestial hall.

'Why did the comet break up?' one said,
'Because it found another to be wed!'
Another one giggled, 'That's just a phase,'
They all cracked up in their asteroid ways.

Through the void, they gather and share,
Meteoroids glimmer without a care.
With every collision, they laugh and collide,
Creating a ruckus on this starry ride.

An asteroid named Chuck told a joke,
'Why did the stardust always provoke?
Because it wanted to be part of a scene,
In the cosmic limelight, it caused quite a sheen!'

Dark Matter Dialogues

In the unknown, whispers abound,
Dark matter speaks without a sound.
'What's heavier than a black hole's might?'
'A bad pun in a cosmic light!'

Invisible friends with a playful air,
Joking, 'Can you see us? We're always there!'
They giggle and wiggle in gravitational pulls,
Mixing humor with cosmic rules.

A photon quipped, 'I'm really quite fast,
But all this chatter, I'll never outlast!'
While neutrinos chimed in with glee,
'We float right through, can you see me?'

In the void of space, laughter can sing,
Among the shadows, the jokes take wing.
'Cause even in darkness, there's fun to find,
In the dialogues of the quirkily inclined!

Whirling Whispers

Spinning planets share their tease,
'When do meteors have time to sneeze?'
A twirling star giggles at that joke,
While orbiting moons merely poke.

Spirals whirl like gossip in the breeze,
Murming to galaxies, 'You'll never believe!'
A cosmic dance in a raucous flow,
Where whimsy ignites every cosmic show.

'Why do comets love a tail?' they cheer,
'For the look and the style, my dear!'
As they spiral through in a jovial trance,
Creating a nebula of laughter's dance.

'Our universe is filled with hearty laughs,
Even black holes play like little staff!'
Whirling whispers float through the night,
In the cosmos, joy is everyone's delight!

Cosmic Conversations

In the dark where stars collide,
Planets giggle, they confide.
A comet flirts with asteroids,
Spilling secrets, making noise.

Black holes laugh, they pull a prank,
While satellites are in the bank.
Martians whisper, 'What a show!'
While Venus blushes, acting slow.

Uranus jokes, 'It's just my ring,'
As little moons around him swing.
Pluto grumbles, 'I'm still a star,'
While cosmic dust dances afar.

Quasar Quips

A quasar winks from far away,
And tells the stars, 'Let's play all day.'
Brightly colored supernova,
Says, 'I'm brighter! It's not over!'

Alien life cracks a joke,
While meteors trail like smoke.
'What's it like to be a sun?'
'Hot and bright – it's just plain fun!'

Asteroids tumble, sharing puns,
Comets race, oh what a run!
In this vast and lively space,
All the cosmos finds its place.

Meteoric Musings

Meteor showers bring delight,
Shooting stars dance through the night.
Saturn spins, a twirling tease,
While nebulae go 'Oh, please!'

Pulsars tick with jokes so quick,
Their rhythm makes us laugh and tick.
Galaxies swirl in a comic twirl,
Making space a funny world.

Pluto says, 'I need a friend,'
But Venus just won't comprehend.
In the cosmic chatty spree,
Laughter echoes endlessly.

Celestials in Cacophony

Celestial beings in a whirl,
Jupiter yells, 'Give it a twirl!'
Stars combine with playful shout,
Creating a ruckus, full of clout.

Mercury zips, what a thrill!
'Catch me if you can, I will!'
Neptunian whispers float and glide,
While cosmic winds take them for a ride.

Galactic jokes fly, bold and bright,
'Who turned off the cosmic light?'
As orbits giggle in their dance,
Creating chaos in a trance.

Astral Curiosities

In space, the stars have a tea,
With comets spilling their glee.
Planets trade jokes on the fly,
While asteroids wink as they pass by.

Saturn gave Mars a haircut,
Venus just laughed, saying, "What!"
Neptune is known for its pranks,
Uranus just rolled, giving thanks.

Black holes are bouncers, quite stout,
They never let anyone out.
Galaxies shuffle, a dance so grand,
While quasars are stunning, just as planned.

The sun plays the role of the clown,
Chasing shadows around town.
And while the Earth tries to keep cool,
The Milky Way's the funniest school.

Constellation Confessions

Orion claims he's a hero,
But his belt is all just a zero.
Cassiopeia stares in the glass,
Saying, "Every star is a class!"

Taurus and Leo have a beef,
Over who brings the most grief.
Gemini giggles, causing a scene,
While Cancer just crabs, feeling mean.

Virgo's always checking the time,
Lamenting her plans don't rhyme.
Pisces swims by with a wink,
Making sure no one can think.

With secrets spotted in the dark,
The constellations crack a spark.
Talk of romance, and who's a star,
In the cosmos, they laugh from afar.

Lunar Legends

The moon spins tales of old fights,
Over cheese with Martian sights.
The sun just laughs, rolls on by,
"Your legends are boring," it'll sigh.

Wolves howl tales by moonlight's glare,
While crickets share a cosmic dare.
Fairies dance on the lunar beams,
Concocting ever far-out dreams.

Aliens plan trips with their pals,
To raid the craters for giggles and gals.
While astronauts chuckle, looking at rocks,
Saying it's just a moonlit box.

Luna grins, a cheeky old sprite,
Playing tricks on this starry night.
And all the stars join in the jest,
Making the universe laugh the best!

Milky Way Murmurs

Whispers float in the starry sea,
Where black holes sip cosmic tea.
Pulsars giggle, blink, and twinkle,
While supernovae rumble and crinkle.

The Milky Way's a bustling street,
With cosmic critters bustling on feet.
Astro-kittens chasing light,
Frolicking through the velvet night.

Galactic gossip floats on by,
"Did you see Jupiter's eye?"
With meteors sharing, "Secret's tight!
We danced on stardust, felt so right!"

Bright stars blush in the Milky glow,
While comets paint their tails in a show.
In this spiral, mirth is the key,
As galaxies giggle joyfully free.

www.ingramcontent.com/pod-product-compliance
Lightning Source LLC
Chambersburg PA
CBHW072145200426
43209CB00051B/458